D1283749

COUNTRY ⊕ PROFILES

SPAIN

BY AMY RECHNER

BLASTOFF!
DISCOVERY

BELLWETHER MEDIA • MINNEAPOLIS, MN

Blastoff! Discovery launches
a new mission: reading to learn.
Filled with facts and features, each
book offers you an exciting new
world to explore!

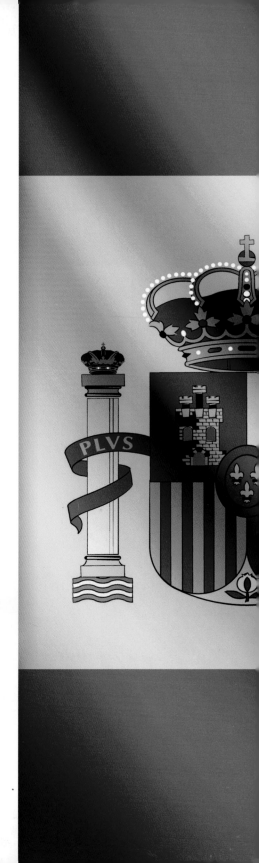

This edition first published in 2019 by Bellwether Media, Inc.

No part of this publication may be reproduced in whole or in part
without written permission of the publisher.
For information regarding permission, write to Bellwether Media, Inc.,
Attention: Permissions Department,
6012 Blue Circle Drive, Minnetonka, MN 55343.

Library of Congress Cataloging-in-Publication Data

Names: Rechner, Amy, author.
Title: Spain / by Amy Rechner.
Description: Minneapolis, MN : Bellwether Media, Inc., 2019. |
    Series: Blastoff! Discovery: Country Profiles | Includes
    bibliographical references and index.
Identifiers: LCCN 2018000620 (print) | LCCN 2018000710 (ebook)
    | ISBN 9781626178441 (hardcover : alk. paper) | ISBN
    9781681035857 (ebook)
Subjects: LCSH: Spain–Juvenile literature.
Classification: LCC DP17 (ebook) | LCC DP17 .R39 2019 (print) |
    DDC 946–dc23
LC record available at https://lccn.loc.gov/2018000620

Editor: Rebecca Sabelko   Designer: Brittany McIntosh

Printed in the United States of America, North Mankato, MN.

TABLE OF CONTENTS

THE TOWERING TEMPLE

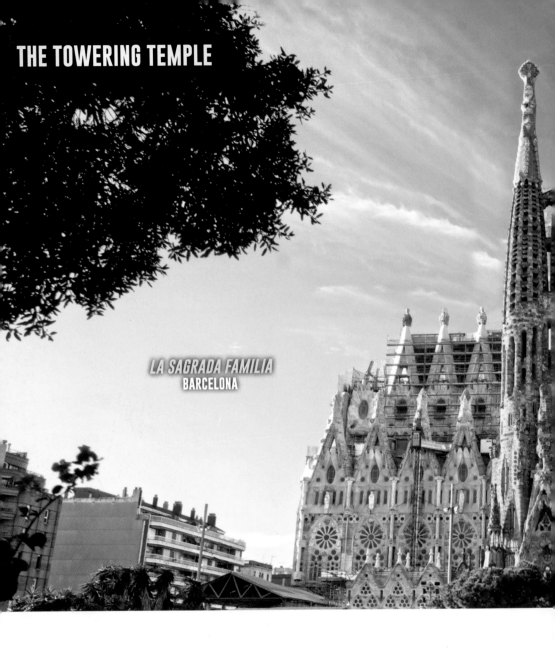

LA SAGRADA FAMILIA
BARCELONA

In Barcelona, a family walks along one of the world's oldest Roman walls. They are on their way to *La Sagrada Familia*, church of the Holy Family. The church has been under construction since 1882. The family stares up at the church's high towers. There will be 18 when it is complete. The tallest will be a **symbol** for Jesus Christ.

OTHER TOP SITES

CATEDRAL DE SANTIAGO DE COMPOSTELA

HERMITAGE OF SAN JUAN DE GAZTELUGATXE

MUSEO DEL PRADO

REAL ALCAZAR

Inside, tall columns branch overhead like trees. Light streams through colorful windows. The magic of the church spreads throughout the city. The family tries to decide their next adventure. There is so much to explore in Spain!

BAY
OF BISCAY

N
W ✛ E
S

PORTUGAL

MADRID

ZARAGOZA

SPAIN

SEVILLE

STRAIT
OF GIBRALTAR

6

AFRICA

FRANCE

ANDORRA

BARCELONA

BALEARIC
ISLANDS

MEDITERRANEAN
SEA

Spain covers 195,124 square miles (505,370 square kilometers) of Western Europe. The capital city of Madrid lies in the center. Spain is on the Iberian **Peninsula** southwest of France. The small country of Andorra is nestled on the French border.

The Bay of Biscay splashes along Spain's northern border. The Mediterranean Sea wraps around the eastern and southern coasts. Spain's Balearic Islands lie within these waters. A narrow waterway called the Strait of Gibraltar separates Spain's southern tip from northern Africa. Portugal is Spain's only land neighbor to the west. Spain's Canary Islands lie off Africa's western coast in the Atlantic Ocean.

LANDSCAPE AND CLIMATE

Spain's largest **plateau** is the Meseta Central. It is surrounded by mountains. The jagged Pyrenees separate Spain from the rest of Europe. The Iberian peaks line the eastern coast toward the Sierra Morena Mountains to the south. The Green Coast's rocky cliffs fall into forested hills and green valleys along the northwest.

N
W + E
S

☐ = MESETA CENTRAL   ☐ = GREEN COAST
☐ = SIERRA MORENA   ☐ = PYRENEES
    MOUNTAINS   MOUNTAINS

MESETA CENTRAL PLATEAU

OTAL VALLEY, PYRNEES MOUNTAINS
SOBRARBE

MADRID
Average seasonal highs and lows

JANUARY
HIGH: 50 °F (10 °C)
LOW: 34 °F (1 °C)

APRIL
HIGH: 63 °F (17 °C)
LOW: 41 °F (5 °C)

JULY
HIGH: 91 °F (33 °C)
LOW: 61 °F (16 °C)

OCTOBER
HIGH: 70 °F (21 °C)
LOW: 48 °F (9 °C)

°F = degrees Fahrenheit
°C = degrees Celsius

The mountains of northern Spain are often humid. They have heavy rainfall and mild temperatures. The Meseta's windswept plains endure extreme heat and cold with little rain. While the Mediterranean coast has dry, hot summers and mild winters, southern Spain's desert-like climate is similar to north Africa.

9

WILDLIFE

The wildlife of Spain is as varied as its **terrain**. In the north, Iberian wolves track down deer in the forests, and Barbastelle bats rest in the loose bark of trees. Eurasian eagle-owls race for prey and bearded vultures circle overhead while brown bears search for berries in the Pyrenees Mountains.

Rare Iberian lynx hunt for rabbits in the Mediterranean **shrubland**. Iberian wild goats graze the rocky southern coasts. Wild boar and Spanish imperial eagles hunt in nearby mountains. Tuna, octopus, and swordfish swim where the Mediterranean and Atlantic meet. The ocean waters are filled with animals like striped dolphins and long-finned pilot whales.

IBERIAN WOLF

BARBASTELLE BAT

EURASIAN EAGLE-OWL

STRIPED DOLPHIN

BEARDED VULTURE

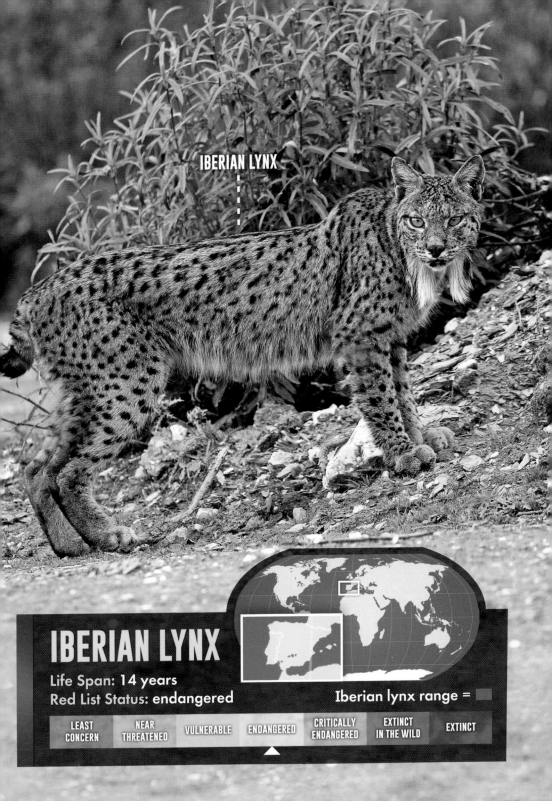

IBERIAN LYNX

IBERIAN LYNX

Life Span: 14 years
Red List Status: endangered

Iberian lynx range =

LEAST CONCERN	NEAR THREATENED	VULNERABLE	ENDANGERED	CRITICALLY ENDANGERED	EXTINCT IN THE WILD	EXTINCT

SPANISH SOUNDS

Castilian Spanish is spoken throughout Latin America, too. However, "s" sounds in Latin America are spoken with a "th" sound in Spain.

Almost 49 million people live in Spain. They have roots in both Europe and northern Africa. Over hundreds of years, different **ethnic** groups have come to Spain. The Catholic Church is an important part of Spanish **culture**. Many Spaniards still consider themselves Catholic. Around one-fourth of the people do not take part in any religion.

Each region has its own culture, and some speak different languages. Spaniards speak their region's language as well as the official language, Castilian Spanish. People in **Catalonia**, Galicia, and Basque speak languages that can be very different from Castilian.

FAMOUS FACE

Name: Rafael Nadal Parera
Birthday: June 3, 1986
Hometown: Balearic Islands, Spain
Famous for: He has won 16 Grand Slam titles, 10 French Open titles, a Gold Medal at the 2008 Olympics in men's singles, and a Gold Medal at the 2016 Olympics in men's doubles

SPEAK SPANISH

ENGLISH	SPANISH	HOW TO SAY IT
hello	hola	OH-lah
goodbye	adiós	ah-dee-OHS
please	por favor	pohr fah-VOR
thank you	gracias	grah-SEE-ahs
yes	sí	SEE
no	no	noh

BENIDORM

COMMUNITIES

Many Spaniards live in **urban** areas, especially around Madrid and Barcelona. They live in small apartments and townhouses. **Suburban** families enjoy bigger homes. Spanish families are often small, with one or two children.

MADRID

14

ZAHARA DE LA SIERRA
ANDALUSIA

Country farmhouses built of stone appear amid northern green fields. Small villages of buildings painted white peek out among the hills of **Andalusia**. White-painted villas and flats overlook the beaches. Although city dwellers can walk or take public transport, those living in suburban areas or the country rely on cars or trains.

Spaniards are warm and friendly. Men are greeted with handshakes. Women receive kisses on each cheek. They enjoy social outings with friends. Conversations usually involve a lot of eye contact while standing close to one another.

A typical day in Spain lasts much later than in many other countries. The most well-known custom of Spain is the *siesta*, the mid-afternoon break. While less common in modern life, a traditional siesta runs from 2 to 5 p.m. The work day ends around 8 p.m. Families rarely finish eating dinner before 10 p.m. Evening outings for ice cream or a stroll can last until midnight.

HUMAN TOWERS

At special Catalonian events, groups of people create human towers called *castells*. The people in the towers stand on each other up to ten levels high. A small child climbs to the top and raises an open hand as the final touch.

Children in Spain must attend school from the ages of 6 to 16. Many start with preschool before beginning primary school. At age 12, students begin secondary school, and most continue until they are 18 years old. Students can choose to begin studying a trade or prepare to go to a university.

Workers in Spain have many different kinds of jobs. Farmers grow grains, olives, and fruit. They raise livestock for meat and dairy. Factory workers make clothing, cars, and machinery. They also process food. Most people in Spain have **service jobs**. Many work in **tourism**, banking, or government.

CHEF

FARMER

FAMOUS FIGHTERS

Matadors, the men who fight bulls, are as famous as movie stars in Madrid and Seville.

Soccer is a big part of Spanish life. Friends get together to cheer Spain's soccer teams, like Real Madrid or FC Barcelona. Children play in soccer and basketball leagues and enjoy playing cards and video games. Spaniards often like to swim, hike, and bike. Many spend time in their gardens and go for strolls.

REAL MADRID

Spaniards like to keep up with popular culture. They enjoy movies, TV, music, and browsing online. Friends often get together in cafes or at public events. During the hot summer months, many head to the beaches or mountains to escape the heat.

CHAPAS

What You Need:
- 2-6 players
- a bottle cap for each player
- a penny for each player
- tape or sticky putty
- plain paper
- scissors
- markers, different colors
- flat surface like a playground, sidewalk, or driveway
- chalk

Instructions:
1. Tape or stick a penny inside each bottle cap for weight.

2. Cut out a circle of paper the same size as the penny. Decorate it and stick it on top of the penny. This is your chapa.

3. Draw a curvy course on the playground, sidewalk, or driveway with chalk. Make sure there is a clear starting line and finish line. The course should be about 6 inches (15 centimeters) wide, but there is no length requirement.

4. Players take turns using one finger to flick their chapas toward the finish line. If you flick your chapa outside of the lines, you lose a turn. If someone flicks their chapa into yours, you must start over. The first player to cross the finish line wins.

TASTE THE TAPAS!

Spaniards often take a break in late morning for *tapas*, tiny plates of delicious food served as snacks. Friends meet and taste the tapas at different places.

Spanish food is full of flavor. Each region has favorite dishes based on what grows there. *Paella*, a rice dish with Mediterranean seafood and vegetables, is popular in eastern Spain. Castilian farms in the north supply beef and ham. *Manchego*, a cheese made of sheep's milk, comes from central Spain. *Gazpacho*, a cold tomato soup, is a southern favorite.

The day starts with a *churro* pastry and coffee with milk. A favorite lunch is salad with roasted garlic chicken and vegetables. Simple desserts include fruit or yogurt. Dinner is light, often a salad and omelet or lunch leftovers. Bread comes with every meal.

MANCHEGO

GAZPACHO

CHOCOLATE CALIENTE

Ingredients:
1 1/2 cups semisweet chocolate chips
2 1/4 cups milk
1 teaspoon cornstarch, dissolved in a little cold water

Steps:
1. With the help of an adult, heat the chocolate chips and the milk in a saucepan.
2. Stir until the chocolate chips are completely melted.
3. When it comes to a boil, add the dissolved cornstarch.
4. Bring to a boil 3 times, whisking quickly and removing from the heat each time it starts to bubble to prevent the mixture from boiling over.
5. Pour into cups and serve immediately.

CELEBRATIONS

Each spring, *Semana Santa*, or Holy Week, is celebrated throughout Spain. The celebrations begin on Palm Sunday. Parades with large floats showing scenes from Jesus' life are carried by people toward churches on Maundy Thursday and Good Friday. All this leads up to the joyful and colorful celebration of Easter Monday.

In March, the *Las Fallas* Festival in Valencia includes giant figures stuffed with ear-shattering fireworks. Seville's *Feria de Abril* in April is filled with the stomping and clapping of *flamenco* dancing. At Pamplona's *Fiesta de San Fermin* in July, bulls chase brave runners through the streets. Spain's many celebrations highlight its **traditions** and culture!

FOOD FIGHT!

In August, a small town in Valencia hosts *La Tomatina*, the world's biggest food fight! Each year, 20,000 people fill the streets to throw tomatoes at each other.

FIESTA DE SAN FERMIN

TIMELINE

711 CE
Muslims from northern Africa gain control of Spain

1588
The British navy defeats the Spanish Armada

218 BCE
Roman troops invade Spain

1492
King Ferdinand and Queen Isabella begin their conquest of new worlds by sending Christopher Columbus in search of a passage to India

1936
The Spanish Civil War begins

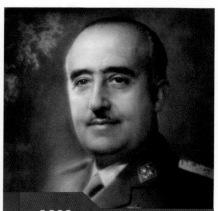

1939

Spanish Civil War ends and Francisco Franco becomes dictator

2004

Ten bombs explode on four trains in Madrid resulting in one of the worst terrorist incidents in Europe since WWII

2017

Catalan citizens try separating Catalonia into an independent nation, but Spain does not let the province go

1975

King Juan Carlos I assumes the throne after Franco dies

2002

Euro replaces peseta due to Spain's membership in European Union

SPAIN FACTS

Official Name: Kingdom of Spain

Flag of Spain: The Spanish flag has two narrow red horizontal stripes at top and bottom, and a wider yellow horizontal stripe in the middle. Spain's coat of arms is pictured on the yellow band, toward the left side.

Area: 195,124 square miles
(505,370 square kilometers)

Capital City: Madrid

Important Cities: Barcelona,
Seville, Zaragoza

Population:
48,958,159 (July 2017)

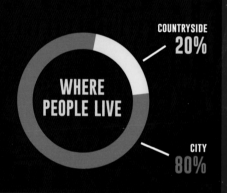

WHERE PEOPLE LIVE

COUNTRYSIDE **20%**

CITY **80%**

MANUFACTURING
24.1%

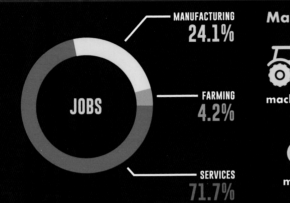

JOBS

FARMING
4.2%

SERVICES
71.7%

Main Exports:

machinery   vehicles   food

medicine   pharmaceuticals

National Holiday:
Hispanic Day, October 12

Main Language:
Spanish

Form of Government:
parliamentary constitutional monarchy

Title for Country Leaders:
prime minister (head of government)
king (head of state)

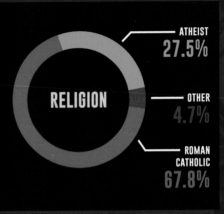

RELIGION

ATHEIST
27.5%

OTHER
4.7%

ROMAN
CATHOLIC
67.8%

Unit of Money:
Euro; 100 cents make up 1 Euro.

GLOSSARY

Andalusia—a southwestern region of Spain

Catalonia—the northeastern region of Spain that borders France and the Mediterranean Sea

culture—the beliefs, arts, and ways of life in a place or society

ethnic—related to a group of people who share customs and an identity

peninsula—a section of land that extends out from a larger piece of land and is almost completely surrounded by water

plateau—an area of flat, raised land

service jobs—jobs that perform tasks for people or businesses

shrubland—dry land that has mostly shrubs

suburban—relating to an area of homes close to or surrounding a city

symbol—something that stands for something else

terrain—the surface features of an area of land

tourism—the business of people traveling to visit other places

traditions—customs, ideas, or beliefs handed down from one generation to the next

urban—related to cities and city life

TO LEARN MORE

AT THE LIBRARY

Ganeri, Anita. *Journey Through Spain*. London, UK: Hachette Children's, 2017.

Mattern, Joanne. *Spain*. New York, N.Y.: Cavendish Square, 2017.

Rechner, Amy. *France*. Minneapolis, Minn.: Bellwether Media, 2018.

ON THE WEB

Learning more about Spain is as easy as 1, 2, 3.

1. Go to www.factsurfer.com.

2. Enter "Spain" into the search box.

3. Click the "Surf" button and you will see a list of related web sites.

With factsurfer.com, finding more information is just a click away.

INDEX

The images in this book are reproduced through the courtesy of: Madrugada Verde, front cover; Luciano Mortula-LGM, pp. 4-5; FCG, p. 5 (top); Landscape Nature Photo, p. 5 (middle top); milosk50, p. 5 (middle bottom); Cezary Wojtkowski, p. 5 (bottom); blickwinkel/ Alamy, p. 8; Jose Manuel Gavira, p. 9 (top); vichie81, p. 9 (bottom); Karel Bartik, p. 10 (left); Alfredo Garcia, p. 10 (top); Real PIX, p. 10 (middle top); Milan Zygmunt, p. 10 (middle bottom); Gonzalo Jara, p. 10 (bottom); Philip Mugridge/ Alamy, p. 11; Tim Graham/ Alamy, p. 12; Storms Media Group/ Alamy, p. 13 (top); Veja, p. 13 (bottom); IR Stone, p. 14; Marques, p. 15; Iakov Filimonov, p. 16; Prisma by Dukas Presseagentur GmbH/ Alamy, p. 17; xavierarnau, p. 18; Mikhail Zahranichny, p. 19 (top); JulieanneBirch, p. 19 (bottom); Angel Simon, p. 20 (top); Christian Bertrand, p. 20 (bottom); Tutti Frutti, p. 21; AWL Images/ Getty, p. 22; BigKnell, p. 23 (top); NSphotostudio, p. 23 (middle); viennetta, p. 23 (bottom); David Ramos/Stringer/ Getty, p. 24; Migel, p. 25; Unknown/ Wikipedia, zp. 26 (top); Eugene Delacroix/ Wikipedia, p. 26 (bottom); Unknown/ Wikipedia, p. 27 (top); Irekia/ Wikipedia, p. 27 (bottom left); Marian Weyo, p. 27 (bottom right); Alan Bauman, p. 29 (currency); Andrey Lobachev, p. 29 (coin).